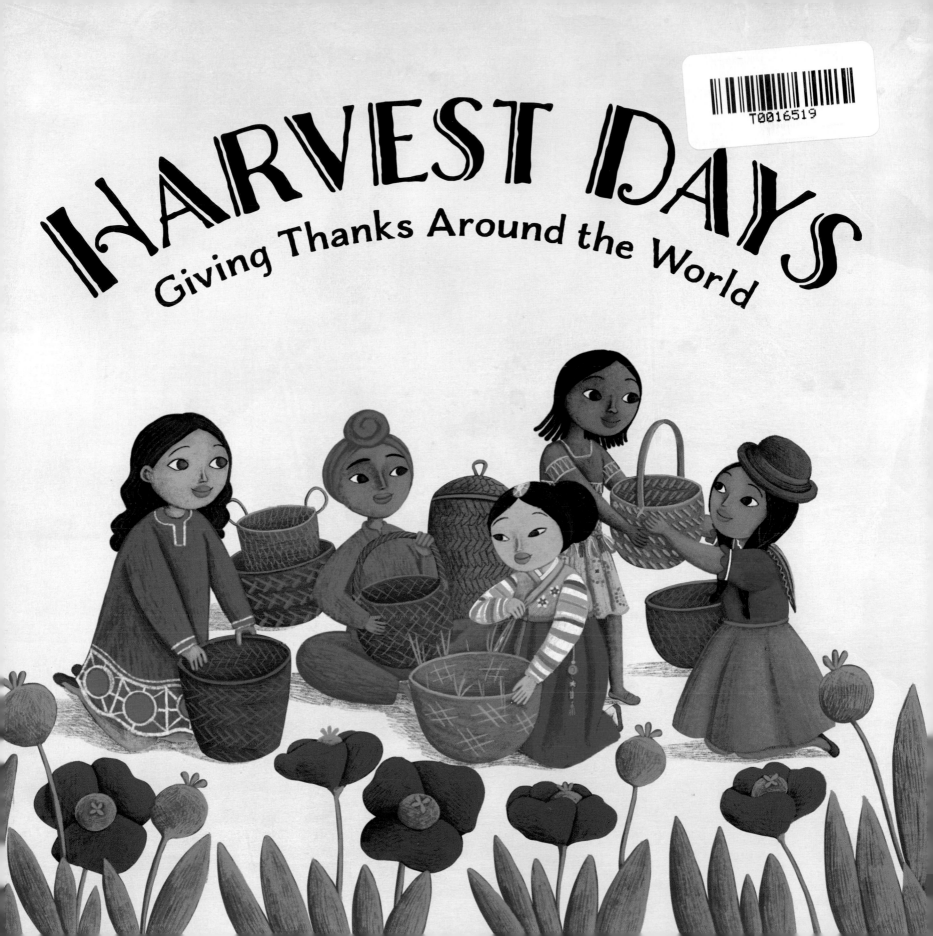

HARVEST DAYS

Giving Thanks Around the World

There are so many celebrations and traditions in the world —
more than one person could experience in a lifetime, and far
more than one book can contain. Not everyone from a culture
or a faith observes the same traditions or celebrates the
same special days. Some traditions span many countries
and cultures. There's a big world beyond this book.

Barefoot Books
23 Bradford Street, 2nd Floor
Concord, MA 01742

Barefoot Books
29/30 Fitzroy Square
London, W1T 6LQ

Text copyright © 2022 by Kate DePalma
Illustrations copyright © 2022 by Martina Peluso
The moral rights of Kate DePalma and Martina Peluso have been asserted

First published in the United States of America by Barefoot Books, Inc
and in Great Britain by Barefoot Books, Ltd in 2022
All rights reserved

Graphic design by Elizabeth Jayasekera, Barefoot Books
Edited and art directed by Autumn Allen, Barefoot Books
Reproduction by Bright Arts, Hong Kong. Printed in China
This book was typeset in Charcuterie Deco, Charcuterie Filigree,
Charcuterie Flared, Duper and Filson Pro
The illustrations were prepared using digital techniques

Hardback ISBN 978-1-64686-626-7 • Paperback ISBN 978-1-64686-627-4
E-book ISBN 978-1-64686-703-5

British Cataloguing-in-Publication Data: a catalogue record
for this book is available from the British Library

Library of Congress Cataloging-in-Publication Data
is available under LCCN 2022936062

3 5 7 9 8 6 4

HARVEST DAYS
Giving Thanks Around the World

written by **Kate DePalma**

illustrated by **Martina Peluso**

Barefoot Books
step inside a story

People as far back as anyone's known
Have gathered to give thanks for food we have grown.

A bountiful harvest is perfect to share.
What a wonderful way to show others you care!

South Korea

When summer is ending and leaves will fall soon,
We gather for Chuseok* beneath a full moon.

*Pronounced CHU-sok

We roll sticky songpyeon* together with speed.
We all love the ones stuffed with sesame seeds!
*Pronounced SONG-pyon

To celebrate the harvest festival of **Chuseok**, families in Korea make rice flour cakes called songpyeon.

Poland

When Dożynki* comes and we cut the last sheaf
We tie it with flowers and make a big wreath.

*Pronounced *do-ZHEN-kee*

At the Slavic festival of **Dożynki**, the last sheaf of grains to be harvested is woven into a wreath and carried in a procession.

We offer the grains and the loaves of fresh bread,
Giving thanks we have food for the cold days ahead.

Tamil Nadu, India

On the third day of Pongal*, we thank all the cows
And the powerful bulls who work hard pulling plows.

*Pronounced *PON-gull*

Pongal is a Hindu harvest festival celebrated by Tamil people in parts of India such as Tamil Nadu. The third day, called **Mattu Pongal**, thanks farm animals for the help they give people.

We dress up the cattle and hand-feed them treats.
The pot's boiling over with sweet rice to eat!

Bolivia

Martes de Challa* is quite a display!
We thank the Earth Mother on Carnival Day.
*Pronounced MAR-tays day CHAI-yah

We offer up water as fireworks crack.
Our planet provides so we want to give back!

On **Martes de Challa**, which falls on the last day of the Carnival season, Bolivians make an offering to the Earth Mother Pachamama, who has been worshipped in the Andes since ancient times.

Ghana

At Homowo* each year, the Gã people recall
Dry days in the past when the harvest was small.
*Pronounced hoe-MOE-woe

Now, laughing at hunger, we all dance and sing.
We're thankful for rain and the harvest it brings.

At **Homowo**, the Gã people of Ghana laugh at hunger and remember when they overcame starvation.

Our ancestors sighed with relief in the sun
Once the back-breaking work of the harvest was done.

Enslaved Africans were brought to Barbados against their will to work on sugarcane plantations. **Crop Over** was born from the relief they felt at the end of the brutal harvest season.

When Crop Over comes, we wear feathers and crowns.
We take pride in our heritage, passing it down.

Morocco

When it's time for Sukkot*, the building we make
Is nice to spend time in, asleep or awake.

*Pronounced *soo-COAT*

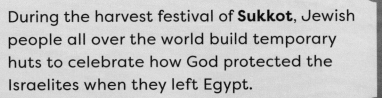

During the harvest festival of **Sukkot**, Jewish people all over the world build temporary huts to celebrate how God protected the Israelites when they left Egypt.

Our family and friends come to meet us inside,
Grateful for all that HaShem can provide.

*Pronounced *ha-SHEM*

Liberia

Each year in November comes Thanksgiving Day.
We show that we're grateful in all different ways.

Some bring fruit to the church and then hear pastors preach,
And others enjoy a fun day at the beach!

Many Liberians attend church services on **Thanksgiving Day** and donate fruit, vegetables and livestock to raise money for the church community. Others who don't celebrate enjoy a day off!

Iran

Our Mehregan* table has flowers and bread,
Some candles, a mirror and fruit that is red.

*Pronounced MEH-reh-gone

We joyfully toss herbs and seeds in the air,
Embracing to show one another we care.

Mehregan is observed every October in Iran by decorating a sofreh (table) with special items, including produce from the harvest.

It's La Tomatina*! Tomatoes are ripe.
Let's head to the streets for a rowdy food fight!

*Pronounced LAH toe-mah-TEE-nah

Every summer, people flock to the small town of Buñol, Spain for **La Tomatina**, a friendly food fight using tomatoes too ripe to be sold.

When tomatoes start flying, you all better run!
But don't throw them too hard — it's only for fun.

Punjab, India

We harvest the wheat when we feel fresh spring air.
Vaisakhi* is here, and it's time for the fair.

*Pronounced *vai-SAH-kee*

The mela* puts us in a jovial mood.
We love all the dancing, the rides and good food!

*Pronounced MAY-lah

At **Vaisakhi** people of all faiths celebrate the winter wheat harvest in Punjab, India. People enjoy having extra money from the harvest to spend on treats at a mela (fair).

Every Saint Martin's Day brings a parade.
We march through the streets with the lanterns we made!

We all sing together by candlelight glow.

Stars twinkle above and we twinkle below.

Christians in Germany celebrate **Saint Martin's Day** every November 11 with a lantern-lit walk that is sometimes led by a man on horseback dressed as Saint Martin.

People have changed how we live through the years
But we still come together when harvest time nears.

We give thanks for our Earth and the hard work that's done
To grow the world's harvests to feed everyone.

Calendar of Harvest Festivals

Mehregan
Iran
October 8

Mattu Pongal
Tamil Nadu, India
around January 16

Vaisakhi
Punjab, India
around
April 13 or 14

Homowo
Ghana
August

Dożynki
Poland
Autumn Equinox

Saint Martin's Day
Germany
November 11

| JANUARY | FEBRUARY | MARCH | APRIL | MAY | JUNE | JULY | AUGUST | SEPTEMBER | OCTOBER | NOVEMBER | DECEMBER |

Martes de Challa
Bolivia
February or March

Crop Over
Barbados
June until the first Monday in August

La Tomatina
Spain
last Wednesday in August

Thanksgiving
Liberia
first Thursday in November

Chuseok
South Korea
September or October

Sukkot
Morocco
September or October

Some of the cultures in this book use their own calendars. That is why some of these special days don't fall on the same day each year according to this calendar.

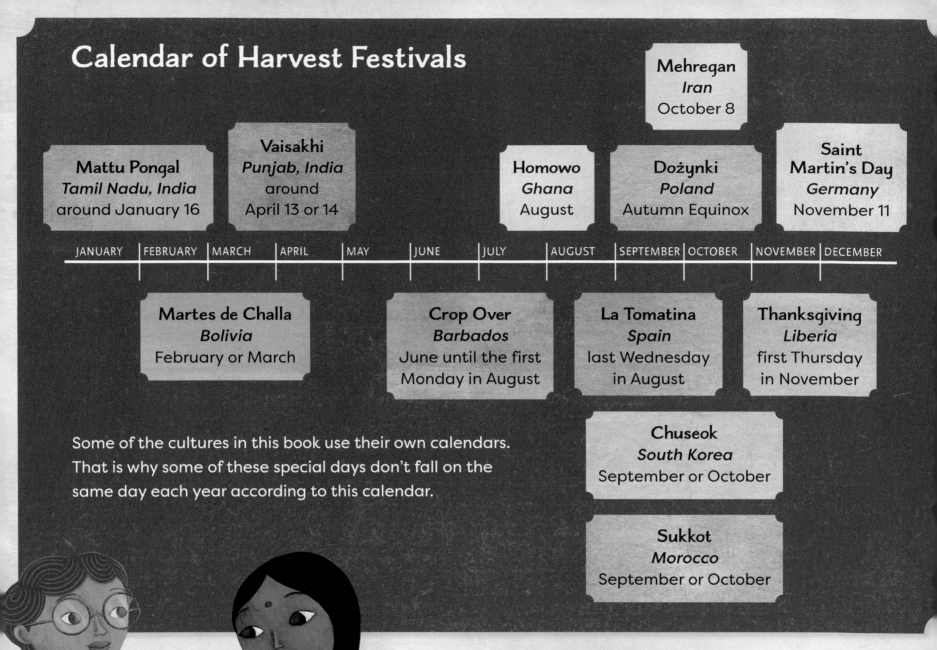

What is the harvest season?

Harvest season comes when the foods we grow are ripe and ready to be gathered. Different crops are harvested at different times, so harvest seasons happen throughout the year around the world.

Why do people celebrate the harvest season?

We rely on harvested food to survive. For farmers, harvest season requires some of the most difficult work of the entire year. After the harvest, there is plenty of food and the farm workers are ready for a break. It's a natural time to gather, celebrate and share.

How have harvest traditions changed through time?

Many people do not experience a strong connection to nature and the seasons, because most people do not grow the food they eat anymore. Some harvest traditions are still celebrated despite having very little connection left to harvesting crops.

Some harvest festivals have been celebrated for so long that they have spread around the world over time. People move around the world for many reasons, taking their traditions with them to their new homes.

Learn and Discover!

If you don't know the answers to some of these questions, ask a grown-up to help you research and find out more:

- How does your culture celebrate the harvest season?
- What foods grow near you? What time of year are they harvested? Have you ever tried eating them?
- Pick one food you like. Where does it grow? How far does it travel to get to you? Who harvests it?

Chuseok in South Korea

- **Chuseok** (*CHU-sok*) is a festival celebrated in North and South Korea at the beginning of autumn on a full moon.

- The harvest is believed to be a blessing from ancestors or relatives who lived long ago. Some families gather to remember and make offerings to their ancestors and to tend to the graves of loved ones. Then traditional foods and games are enjoyed.

- Many families make sticky rice flour cakes called **songpyeon** (*SONG-pyon*). They contain different fillings like sesame seeds and honey, soybeans, red beans, chestnuts and dates. Then they are steamed over pine needles.

- Some people enjoy wearing traditional Korean clothes called **hanbok** (*HAN-bok*) at Chuseok.

Dożynki in Poland

- **Dożynki** (*do-ZHEN-kee*) is a harvest festival celebrated by Slavs, a group of people who live in parts of Europe and Asia. The celebration falls on different dates in different Slavic nations. In Poland, it is celebrated in September, on the Autumn Equinox. The celebration dates back thousands of years to pre-Christian times, though today some Dożynki celebrations are organized by churches.

- The last sheaf (bundle) of grains harvested from the fields is made into a wreath. It might be decorated with fruits, vegetables or flowers. Wreaths might be small enough for one person to carry or might be enormous!

- Everyone gathers to march with the wreath and give it as an offering of thanks for the plentiful harvest. Some people wear festive traditional clothes. After the procession, people may enjoy food and dancing.

Mattu Pongal in Tamil Nadu, India

- **Pongal** *(PON-gull)* is a four-day harvest festival celebrated by Tamil people in India to give thanks to the Hindu sun god, Surya. It usually falls around January 16.

- Pongal is also the name of the dish prepared for the event, made with newly harvested rice and dal (lentils) sweetened with a type of sugar called jaggery. It is often cooked outside over a fire in groups as a social event. Pongal means "boil" or "overflow" in Tamil — the way the pongal boils over represents the blessings of the harvest.

- The third day of Pongal, called Mattu Pongal, celebrates the hard work farm animals do that makes the harvest possible, like pulling heavy plows (or ploughs) through the soil. Cows are bathed, decorated and fed pongal as a treat.

- People enjoy eating pongal too! Family and friends gather for music and dancing. People also make bright artwork called **kolam** *(KOH-lam)*, using rice powder to adorn the ground.

Martes de Challa in Bolivia

- **Martes de Challa** *(MAR-tays day CHAI-yah)* is a tradition widespread throughout Bolivia of making an offering or **challa** *(CHAI-yah)* on Shrove Tuesday, the last day of the Christian festive season of Carnival. The challa gives thanks to the Ayamara Earth Mother, Pachamama, for the harvest.

- The Ayamara are an Indigenous people who have lived in Bolivia and other parts of South America for centuries. Hundreds of years ago, they came under the control of the Inka people and later the Spanish people. Some parts of Ayamara culture and traditions have remained intact, and some parts have mixed with Catholic traditions brought by Spanish colonists.

- Offerings include sweets, confetti, balloons, flowers and curly streamers called **serpentina** *(ser-pen-TEE-nah)*. Celebrations include playing with water and lighting fireworks — even noise is an offering to Pachamama!

Homowo in Ghana

- **Homowo** *(hoe-MOE-woe)* means "hoot at hunger" in the Gã language spoken by the Gã people of Ghana. The annual Homowo harvest festival remembers a time when there was not enough rain to grow crops and the Gã people had to survive without enough to eat. Now that they have plenty to eat, the Gã people gather each year to laugh at the idea of hunger. The tradition has also come to be a celebration of peace.

- The Gã people prepare a special dish called **kpekpele** *(peck-PEL-eh)* or **kpokpoi** *(POCK-poi)*, for Homowo. It is made with cornmeal, palm nut soup and smoked fish.

- It is tradition to sprinkle some of the kpekpele on the ground as an offering to ancestors. This is done by the head of the household at home and also in public by local leaders.

- During Homowo, people enjoy marching through the streets singing and dancing. Many wear festive red clothing.

Crop Over in Barbados

- **Crop Over** is a harvest festival that originated on sugarcane plantations in Barbados. For centuries, African people were captured and brought to the Americas against their will to perform brutal work for no pay. Crop Over was a way for enslaved Africans to release some of the pain and tension at the end of the cruel harvest season and to express certain aspects of their spirituality.

- Crop Over does not revolve around eating food, because the enslaved people on the sugarcane plantations didn't get to eat the food they harvested. Instead, people had to celebrate with what they had — their voices and their bodies — so Crop Over focuses instead on singing, dancing and other performances.

- There are two months of Crop Over parades, music, parties, costumes, artwork, dancing, food and more! The finale is the Grand Kadooment on the first Monday in August. Children can enjoy a special event just for them called Junior Kadooment. Both are parades featuring groups called Masquerade Bands in elaborate costumes. It is a time for families to reunite and for Barbadian culture and traditions to be passed from one generation to the next. Costumes are often handmade with great care by loved ones.

Sukkot in Morocco

- The Jewish festival of **Sukkot** *(soo-COAT)* is celebrated in September or October. It takes place over seven days in Israel and eight days in the rest of the world. Jewish people have lived all over the world for thousands of years. This is known as the Jewish diaspora.

- People build a temporary structure called a **sukkah** *(soo-KAH)*. This tradition remembers how God protected the ancient Israelites when they left Egypt. Sukkahs are at least 3ft (1m) tall. They have a roof that is open to the sky and made of organic materials from the ground (plants). Families and communities build them together, then enjoy eating and sometimes sleeping inside.

- Sukkahs in different regions of the world often look different. Morrocan sukkahs might feature the bright, detailed fabrics Morocco is famous for. Jewish people have lived in Morocco since ancient times, where there was once a Jewish population of 300,000 people. Today Moroccan Jews live all over the world, especially Israel, where they make up the second-largest Jewish community. This scene is set in Morocco to highlight the diverse array of Jewish diaspora traditions.

- **HaShem** *(ha-SHEM)* means "The Name" in Hebrew, and is used to refer to God.

Thanksgiving Day in Liberia

- In the late 1800s, a group called the American Colonization Society bought land in western Africa because they wanted to send Americans of African descent away. The settlements that formed eventually united into Liberia.

- Many of the first emigrants to Liberia were from families that had lived in the United States for generations. These emigrants brought American traditions with them, including the harvest tradition of Thanksgiving, which became an official holiday in Liberia in 1883. Like the American tradition, Liberian Thanksgiving comes every November, but Liberia celebrates Thanksgiving in its own way.

- Liberia has faced many struggles and conflicts, so Thanksgiving is a day of gratitude that the nation has remained stable for another year.

- It is traditional to make donations of fruits, vegetables or livestock to churches or mosques. These items are blessed and auctioned off to raise money for the congregation. For many, prayer is central to Thanksgiving.

- Many younger people choose to use the day off work and school to relax at the beach, since much of the Liberian population lives near the coast.

Mehregan in Iran

- **Mehregan** *(MEH-reh-gone)* is a Zoroastrian and Iranian festival celebrating the divinity Mithra. Many people call it the Persian Festival of Autumn and it falls on October 8 in Iran. Mehregan has been celebrated in Iran for thousands of years. (Persia is another name for Iran.)

- On Mehregan, people wear new clothes and set a decorative table called a **sofreh** *(SOH-freh)*. The sofreh is covered with crops from the harvest, including red fruits, herbs, nuts, sweets and bread. It might also include a mirror, flowers, candles, water, frankincense, a Zoroastrian religious text called *Kordeh Avesta* and sormeh, a dark substance that is applied around the eyes as makeup.

- Celebrations include praying in front of the mirror, darkening the eyes with sormeh, dancing, embracing and showering loved ones with herbs and seeds.

- Long ago, Zoroastrianism was the state religion of Persia, but then Islamic Arabs conquered Persia, so today Muslims make up the majority of the Iranian population. Mehregan is one of many pre-Islamic traditions that is still celebrated throughout Iran.

La Tomatina in Spain

- In 1945, at a parade in **Buñol** *(bun-YALL)*, Spain, a group of young people got into an argument. Someone threw a soft, overripe tomato from a fruit stand and it became an all-out tomato fight. People had so much fun that they brought tomatoes back every year to keep the tradition going. Local officials tried to stop the gathering, but it was too popular. The annual tomato fight on the last Wednesday in August grew from a local tradition to an international event.

- Tens of thousands of people travel every year to the small town of Buñol for **La Tomatina** *(LAH toe-mah-TEE-nah)*. The friendly tomato fight leaves the participants covered in messy red tomato pulp from head to toe! Participants throw over 150,000 overripe tomatoes, which are brought in on trucks.

- People have raised concerns about this tradition, saying that it is a waste of food. The tomatoes used for La Tomatina are close to rotting and not considered to be safe for humans to eat.

Vaisakhi in Punjab, India

- **Vaisakhi** (or Baisakhi) *(vai-SAH-kee or bai-SAH-kee)* is an ancient springtime harvest festival from the Punjab region of India. The festival celebrates the solar new year and the harvest of the winter grains.

- Traditionally, in farming communities, people gather to help one another harvest the wheat from the fields. Workers come from other states as well. After the harvest is in and sold, the work is done and people have money to spend on having fun. So it's a natural time to have a fair or a **mela** *(MAY-lah)*. Melas include food, shopping, entertainment, rides and more! People perform the traditional **bhangra** *(BAHNG-gruh)* dance with energetic jumps and kicks.

- Vaisakhi is celebrated by all faiths, but the majority of people in Punjab are from the Sikh faith. Vaisakhi has special meaning for Sikhs as the day they remember the birth of the Khalsa in 1699, which transformed the Sikh faith. Many Sikhs have left Punjab and settled in other parts of the world, bringing the tradition of Vaisakhi with them. For example, Vaisakhi is the largest annual single-day event in Vancouver, Canada.

Saint Martin's Day in Germany

- According to the Christian calendar, Saint Martin's Day comes every year on November 11. The day celebrates Saint Martin of Tours, a French saint best known for cutting his coat in half with his sword to share it with a man who was cold in the winter. The feast day of Saint Martin falls at the end of the autumn harvest season and is celebrated in a number of ways in different countries and cultures.

- In Germany, Saint Martin's Day is celebrated with a lantern-lit parade the night before. Children walk along with their parents singing and carrying homemade lanterns. The procession might be led by someone dressed as Saint Martin riding a horse.

- The procession often ends in the town square with a bonfire. Children enjoy baked treats and goose is the traditional dinner.

The author would like to thank the many people who helped ensure the accuracy of this book, including:

Sarah Aroeste * Tete Cobblah * Dr. Elwood Dunn * Adi Elbaz * Gabriela Fuentes
Dr. Sukhdeep Gill and Dr. Surinder Gill * Branka Ivkovic-Bracht * Amanda Jones
The Kissler Family * Dr. Hae Won Park * Gosia Rotfeld * Bhajneet Singh * Meera Sriram * Eva Stratmann
Alex and Homa Tavangar * Sandra Wobbe * Anne Cohen, disability and inclusivity consultant

Author's Note

Harvest festivals are among the most ancient traditions on Earth. Long before humankind had organized itself into societies with customs and rituals of their own, all we had was the rhythms of the planet. Today, many people feel very little relationship to the seasons that bring us the food we eat. Harvest festivals offer us an opportunity to reconnect to that relationship.

Creating this book, which offers a look at just a few of the endless variety of harvest traditions found on our planet, gave me the opportunity to connect with so many people from around the world to learn more about what harvest means in their cultures. The process gave me a new appreciation for the land that provides our food and the hard work of the people who grow it. I hope reading it does the same for you!

— Kate DePalma

Illustrator's Note

Growing up in Italy, we all looked forward to the summertime tomato harvest and the tradition of making tomato purée that has been handed down for generations. We bought tomatoes in the countryside and then spread them in the sun on blankets to ripen. Once they were ripe, we crushed the tomatoes and canned them in jars to last the year. We often gathered with loved ones to work together, laughing as the scent of tomatoes filled the air.

Creating this artwork gave me a chance to get to know traditions from around the world that were new to me. I spent long hours researching the celebrations to make sure that every dish of food, every item of clothing and every festive detail is an accurate representation of the culture it comes from. I hope this book inspires you to be curious about our big world. Why not go and explore it?

— Martina Peluso